This book is dedicated to all who find Nature not an adversary to conquer and destroy, but a storehouse of infinite knowledge and experience linking man to all things past and present. They know conserving the natural environment is essential to our future well-being.

ACADIA

THE STORY BEHIND THE SCENERY®

by Bill Clark

Bill Clark studied geology at Tufts University and then enjoyed a career as a park ranger. He served at a number of National Parks. Now retired, he lives on Mount Desert Isand, Maine, in the shadow of Acadia National Park. He teaches geology and maritime history for the Acadia Senior College and provides natural and human history education for Elderhostel and College of the Atlantic summer programs.

Acadia National Park, located on the coast of Maine, had its beginnings in 1916, as Sieur de Monts National Monument. In 1919, Congress created Lafayette National Park. In 1929, it was renamed Acadia National Park.

Front cover: Granite shoreline, photo by Glenn Van Nimwegen. Inside front cover: Bass Harbor Head Light, photo by Robert Thayer. Page 1: Bunchberry in bloom, photo by Glenn Van Nimwegen. Pages 2/3: Great Head from Oak Cliffs photo by Glenn Van Nimwegen.

Edited by Maryellen Conner. Book design by K. C. DenDooven.

Tenth Printing, 2010 • Revised Edition

LC 2004101676 . ISBN 978-0-88714-245-1

The rhythms of the ocean are the heartbeat of Acadia.
The waves roll in, inexorably and forever;

the tides keep their own time, every 12 hours and 36 minutes,
forever – ocean and granite, irresistible and immovable.

The Acadia Story

Location, location, location! *Jordan Pond House sits astride a glacial landscape – a moraine, a dam of glacial rubble – holding the water of Jordan Pond. Thomas McIntire and his wife opened a teahouse in 1896. The original old farmhouse building burned in 1979 and was rebuilt in 1982. Generations of Mount Desert Island visitors have enjoyed tea and popovers.*

GLENN VAN NIMWEGEN

"The same day we passed also near and island about four or five leagues long... It is very high, notched in places, so as to appear from the sea like a range of seven or eight mountains close together. The summits of most of them are bar of trees for they are nothing but rock... I named it Island of the Desert Mountains (Isles des Monts Déserts)."

SAMUEL DE CHAMPLAIN'S JOURNAL, SEPTEMBER 5, 1604.

Acadia's carriage roads are gentle paths of wonder providing new vistas and new delights around every gentle curve. The Stanley Brook Bridge is one of seventeen on the 56 miles of carriage road on the island.

N Native Americans were here before Champlain. Then after him came settlers, and then in the mid-1800s, "rusticators." They came for magnificent scenery and unsurpassed opportunities for nature study, rocking (we call it hiking today), canoeing and sailing. They were followed by the great hotel era, and then the rich and famous.

The summer people were ultimately responsible for the creation of a park in 1916, and the magnificent scenery, nature study, hiking, canoeing (and kayaking), and sailing are still available today. An unparalleled network of trails provides access to forest, seascape and mountaintop. The 56 miles of carriage roads are used by hikers, bikers, crosscountry skiers, and for horse drawn carriages. The 20 mile Park Loop Road—and its spur road to the top of Cadillac Mountain—provides motorists with a complete overview of park scenery and park resources. Canoeists and kayakers still enjoy ponds, lakes, and protected coastal waters. Deciduous and evergreen forest provides habitat for a host of animals.

Now and forever, Acadia National Park is one of America's greatest treasures.

We can never know what Acadia's shoreline used to look like. The rugosa rose, a transplant from Asia, has become the dominant seashore species.

*The Cranberry Island Series includes
siltstone since metamorphosed into slate
along with lava, tuff blown out of ancient volcanoes.*

Domes, Glaciers and a Rockbound Coast

VICTOR VAN KEUREN

If there was ever such a meeting place of land and sea, pink granite, the immovable object vs. ceaseless ocean waves, the irresistible force, then it is Acadia. Acadia is a battleground!

The exquisite lakes and ponds, classic U-shaped valleys, and a myriad of other glacial features are evidence of repeated continental glaciations. Acadia is glacial landscape.

But granite sets this exquisite place apart from all other American landscapes. Acadia National Park is granite domes.

PLATE TECTONICS

According to the theory of plate tectonics, crustal plates are the building blocks of the earth's crust.

The earth consists of solid brittle crust, plastic mantle, and solid iron-nickel core. Convection currents within the mantle raft crustal plates across the surface of the globe. The moving plates slide past, collide, and override one another.

Deep sea drilling revealed that oceanic rocks on both sides of the mid-Atlantic Ridge were mirror images of one another, and that rocks on both sides became older and older with increasing distance from the Ridge. The North American and Eurasian plates have been moving away from one another for 180 million years—the approximate age of the Atlantic Ocean.

Schoodic Peninsula lies across Frenchman Bay from *Mount Desert Island. At the "Raven's Nest" the granite forms sheer cliffs. At low tide rounded popplestones are exposed. At high tide waves inexorably undercut the granite cliff - aided and abetted by horizontal and vertical joints in the rock.*

At Monument Cove, the relentless ocean destroys some rocks, merely knocks off the rough edges and rounds others. They used to call the rounded boulders on Maine's coast "popplestones." Transported to the big cities of the east coast, they became "cobblestones," and paved the streets.

THE OLDEST ROCKS

More than 600 myBP (million years Before Present) sands, mud, and volcanic rocks accumulated on a shallow sea floor, possibly a continental shelf. The supercontinent called Pangea was forming. A small nearby subcontinent, Avalonia, began to be overridden by the ancestral North American plate—Avalonia and the sea floor sediments began to disappear under ancestral North America. This subduction continued for some 150 million years. As Avalonia and the seafloor sediments were driven deeper into the earth's crust, pressure and heat increased enough to metamorphose the oceanic sediments into the Ellsworth Schist. Portions of the schist escaped the subduction. Planed off, they were pasted against the edge of North America. Erosion exposed the schist at the surface.

The Bar Harbor Formation and Cranberry Islands Series (420 - 380 myBP) were deposited on a shallow ocean floor over the eroded surface of the Ellsworth Schist. The Bar Harbor Formation is sandstone, siltstone, and volcanic lava and ash, deposited in horizontal layers that have been only mildly deformed in all the geologic time since then. The Cranberry Island Series includes siltstone since metamorphosed into slate along with moten volcanic ash, tuff blown out of ancient volcanoes.

THE GRANITES

Acadia's granites formed between 380 and 360 myBP. Subduction carried Avalonia rocks deeper into the earth's crust and closer to the molten rocks of the mantle. At depth the rocks melted into liquid magma. The pools of magma behaved like balloons, rising in the direction of least pressure—towards the surface. The magma moved up by shoving aside the overlying rocks, melting them, shattering them, and making them part of the magma melt. As the magma moved slowly closer to the surface it cooled and finally solidified into granitic rocks.

Gabbro-diorite is the oldest granitic rock on Mount Desert Island. It is dark colored, rich in the on Mount Desert Island is the granite of Southwest Harbor, dated at 373 myBP, followed by the granite of Cadillac Mountain (365 myBP), and the granite of Somesville. Other granites are those of Baker Island and Bass Harbor Head.

Granite of Cadillac Mountain is light colored and coarse grained. The light colored minerals are glassy quartz and pink or gray feldspar. The most common dark colored mineral is hornblende. This granite is extremely resistant to erosion and forms the mountains of Acadia National Park.

Granite of Somesville outcrops around Somes Sound consists of quartz, feldspar, and biotite (black mica) crystals, rather than the hornblende of the Granite of Cadillac Mountain. While there were more than seventy granite quarries on Mount Desert Island, the granite of choice was the Granite of Somesville—for its quality as a building stone and because of the ease of loading it onto granite schooners in Somes Sound.

As the molten Granite of Cadillac Mountain melted its way toward the surface, it shattered the overlying country rock. Pieces of the overlying rock broke off and fell into the magma, melted, and became part of the mix. As the magma cooled it became more viscous—sticky. Pieces of overlying rock that fell into sticky magma retained their individual characteristics and can be identified as Ellsworth Schist or other older rock. Exceptional shatter zone exposures are at the Schooner Head parking area, on the east side of Sand Beach, and at Little Hunters Beach.

ROBERT THAYER

Black diabase dikes are the result of molten rock filling cracks in Acadia's granite. The fine-grained diabase erodes more easily and faster than the coarse-grained and harder granite country rock.

iron-magnesium minerals and poor in quartz. The gabbro-diorite may have come from melting of iron-magnesium rich oceanic rocks (basalt) that were subducted, or perhaps mantle material from even greater depths. Some molten gabbro-diorite was injected as horizontal sills between layers of the Bar Harbor Formation—these sills form the north facing inclined planes of the Porcupine Islands.

Granite is a light colored rock poor in the dark iron-magnesium minerals and rich in quartz (silica). There were several episodes of granite intrusion. The oldest is the granite on Schoodic Point, dated by isotopic techniques at 377 myBP. Oldest

DIKES

Crisscrossing Mount Desert Island and exposed in spectacular fashion at Schoodic Point are long, narrow outcrops of black rock called dikes. Acadia's rocks were broken by cracks called joints, reaching deep underground. Molten magma—deeper in the earth's crust forced its way into some of these joints and hardened to form diabase dikes. Diabase is a fine grained, dark colored rock. The fine grain indicates a rapid cooling relatively close to the surface. These dikes may have fed volcanoes that have long since eroded away. These dikes are the youngest bedrock on Mount Desert Island.

***M**olten magma forced its way toward the earth's* surface – melting, shattering, enveloping the overlying rock. Jagged blocks of older rock fell into the magma and became a part of it.

VICTOR VAN KEUREN

GLENN VAN NIMWEGEN

***T**he moving glacier sanded and* polished Acadia's granite. In most places, the polish has weathered away. It can still be seen on rocks covered by overlying sediments until recently.

GLACIERS

There have been at least three ice ages in the last 500 million years. More than twenty times in the last two million years—the duration of the current ice age—continental ice sheets have covered the northern latitudes of North America and Eurasia. We live in an interglacial period—a warmer time in between ice sheets.

Glaciers begin as snow fields. When snowfall exceeds snow melt, snow fields grow. As snow depth increases, snow at the bottom changes to ice. When the total depth of the ice and snow reaches about 200 feet, the solid ice becomes plastic—capable of flow. The ice flows in all directions away from its deepest point—eventually becoming a continental glacier.

To have an ice age—a time of continental glaciation—many things have to happen. Some of these things have to do with configurations of land masses on the earth's surface. Others have to do with cyclic variations in the earth's orbit and its angle of tilt towards the sun.

About every 100,000 years the earth's orbit changes from nearly circular to elliptical and back. In a more elliptical orbit the earth gets farther from the sun, reducing the amount of solar energy reaching the earth. About every 41,000 years the tilt of the earth toward the sun varies from 22° to 24.5° —minimum tilt makes polar regions cooler in summer (less melting) and warmer in winter (more

When the glacial ice melted off of Mount Desert Island, the Great Meadow was a great lake. Now it is a bog. Someday it will be a meadow – then a forest. South of the meadow Huguenot Head (left) and Dorr Mountain frame a classic U-shaped glacially carved valley.

The Precipice Trail on the east side of Champlain Mountain is closed in spring and early summer. These cliffs are a favorite nesting place for peregrine falcons, reintroduced to the park in the 1980s.

precipitation). About every 22,000 years the earth completes a wobble—determining whether the Northern Hemisphere will be closer or further from the sun during the summer. When the Northern Hemisphere is further away in summer there will be less melting.

These three motions came together about 100,000 years ago and the Wisconsinan ice sheet covered much of North America. Ice as much as two miles thick covered Mountain Desert Island— ice flowing from north to south and a hundred miles further to the south at the edge of the continental shelf—where it calved into the Atlantic Ocean. The ice melted away from Mount Desert Island 13,000 years ago.

Acadia's surface features are the work of glaciers. The valleys run from north to south—the direction of glacial flow. Glacial striations and chatter marks on the solid granite are oriented north to south. Boulder fields on granite domes are rocks that were once embedded in the ice. The domes are steep on their sides and gently rounded on top be-

cause the ice forced its way through the narrow valleys—widening them and sculpting them into a U-shaped cross section. The mountains are *roche moutonnée* (stone sheep)—gently sanded on the north side toward glacial flow, and steep on the south side as a result of glacial plucking.

The lakes and ponds fill north to south depressions carved by glaciers. Glaciers carry unimaginable amounts of debris—sand and mud, boulders and pebbles. Some lakes and ponds lie behind great dams of glacial till—moraines—left behind when there was a pause, for a few years, in the melting of the glacier.

When ice covered the land, the weight of the ice pressed down the rock beneath, perhaps 300 feet. When the ice melted sea level was about 330 feet lower than it is now. Since then the elastic rock has been slowly rebounding. Remains of beaches and marshes can be found high above the present sea level, and sea caves broken into granite cliffs by pounding waves are on the sides of mountains. Today the glaciers in high latitudes continue to

*B*orn of molten magma, sculpted by ice, The Bubbles overlook Jordan Pond.

melt and sea level continues to rise—slowly—in-undating low places and eroding unconsolidated glacial till exposed at the edge of the sea.

GRANITE DOMES

Glacier National Park and Acadia National Park are glacial landscapes, but they bear little resemblance to one another. At Glacier National Park, valley glaciers carved weaker sedimentary and metamorphic rocks into spectacular angles and peaks. At Acadia the continental glaciers could not carve Acadia's domes. Rather, Acadia's domes successfully resisted the efforts of the ice sheets to destroy them.

Granite Domes are the bedrock of Acadia National Park. Once the granite formed the core of a great mountain range, since eroded away. Because granite is the hardest rock commonly found on the surface, the granite domes remained after their overlying mountains were gone—literally the "Rock of Ages"—lasting some 360 million years so far. As the tremendous weight of the overlying rocks was removed, the granite expanded. When granite expands it cracks along gently curving surfaces that follow the shape of the domes. As surface layers are eroded away—peeled away like the layers of an onion—the dome shape is always maintained. This process is called exfoliation

through load relief.

More than any other feature—more than rocky seashore; more than glacial valley, lake, and pond; more than boreal forests—the granite domes are Acadia National Park.

SUGGESTED READING

GILMAN, RICHARD A. et al. *The Geology of Mount Desert Island: A Visitor's Guide to the Geology of Acadia National Park.* Augusta: Maine Geological Survey, Department of Conservation, 1988.

WESSELS, TOM. *The Granite Landscape: A Natural History of America's Mountain Domes, from Acadia to Yosemite.* Woodstock, VT: The Countryman Press, 2001.

The MASSIVE granite domes remained long after the rest of the mountain fell away.

The Overlooks

Cadillac Mountain, greatest
elevation in the park at 1,530 ft,
looks down on Bar Harbor and Frenchman Bay. The glacial ice flowed north to
south (left to right)—planing the north side, plucking the south side.

ROBERT THAYER

Beech Mountain and Long Pond
are highlights of the west side of
Mount Desert Island—the "back side" or "quiet side." Pitch pine
thrives in the subalpine environment of Acadia's highlands.

ROBERT THAYER

From the sheer face of The Beehive, Acadia's Sand Beach appears in its proper perspective—a tiny beach in a protected cove. Sand Beach consists almost entirely of ground up seashells. A shallow brackish lagoon lies behind the beach.

A glacial pond, The Bowl, lies behind northern gentle side of The Beehive. The backside of The Beehive is deceptively gentle. In 1908 Mrs. Charles B. Homans donated The Bowl and The Beehive, which became the birthplace of Acadia National Park.

LOUIS AGASSIZ

In 1837 the young Swiss naturalist Louis Agassiz astonished the scientific community by announcing that huge glaciers once covered large sections of northern Europe. Astonishment quickly subsided to amusement as the scientists of the day stoutly and derisively rejected this threat to dearly held beliefs. Agassiz would eventually triumph, for the evidence in support of his theory was unshakable, evidence that was scattered all over northern Europe in the form of heaped moraines of sand and gravel, or rock beds grooved and scratched, of displaced boulders, of U-shaped valleys, and many other signatures left by the moving glaciers.

In a few days the water will have evaporated. The subalpine environment on the mountaintops is cold, swept by desiccating winds, and dry. Depressions in the granite conserve life-giving water, and also collect precious wind-borne soil.

GLENN VAN NIMWEGEN

DAVID MUENCH

Bubble Rock rests precariously on the South Bubble. Glaciers are dirty. They carry dust, sand grains, pebbles, and rocks. As the glacier moves, these rock materials are ground smaller and smaller. As the glacier melts, the rock materials are left behind. Bubble Rock came from the Lucerne Hills, some 30 miles to the north. When it started on its journey, it might have been the size of a house.

Agassiz came to America in 1846, took a professorship at Harvard, and taught zoology and geology there for 27 years. After a visit to Maine and Mount Desert Island in 1864, he wrote, in his Geological Sketches: *"Mount Desert... must have been a miniature Spitzbergen, and colossal icebergs floated off from Somes Sound into the Atlantic Ocean, as they do nowadays from Magdalena Bay..."* and: *"We are ... justified in supposing that the icefields, when they poured from the north over New England to the sea, had a thickness of at least five or six thousand feet."*

*Acadia's wildlife is good at avoiding people —
blending into the foliage and periods of dense
ocean fog can make Mount Desert Island
into a Garden of Eden.*

Diversity of Life at Acadia

It all begins with lichens colonizing bare granite. This harebell may have its roots in soil captured from the wind by lichens.

GLENN VAN NIMWEGEN

At Acadia, life is everywhere from the lowest zone of the intertidal zone to the mountaintops.

The moisture-laden fog makes Acadia a lichen paradise. Lichens are the only organisms capable of colonizing bare granite. They create a tiny amount of soil from physical and chemical interactions with individual grains of granite. But they are more effective in capturing dust from the passing wind—the beginnings of soil. Mosses get a start in the shallow soil captured by the lichens, then small plants such as the harebell.

The intertidal zone is as rich as any on earth. Barely above high tide, blue-green algae paint the rock black in the splash zone. The barnacle zone colors the bare rock white and yellow-green – it is under water a few hours each day. Lower still are the seaweed zones, spending only a few hours a day exposed to the atmosphere. Every zone has its own assemblage of different algae and animals. The diversity of intertidal life is incomprehensible - look under any growth of seaweed.

Herring gulls and people have a lot in common—we thrive in almost any environment. The picnic table and the mountaintop are not their natural habitat. Leave no trace.

Herring gulls and people have a lot in common - we thrive in almost any environment.

Herring gulls are omnivorous—they thrive wherever their natural foods occur, and wherever people feed them or discard their trash.

Twice each day the tide recedes, exposing Acadia's shoreline and its incredible beautiful and fragile tide pools, each containing its own rich diversity of life forms. Because of trampling and collecting, tide pools are Acadia's most threatened natural resource.

Acadia blooms in deciduous and coniferous woods, in bog, marsh, and pond, along roadsides and in meadows, and on the dry, rocky mountains. Abundant sunshine, moderate rain, and periods of dense ocean fog make Mount Desert Island a Garden of Eden. Much of this flowering takes place in May and June—and has already passed when most vacationers arrive. But in July there is an assemblage of flowers and in August it is berry month.

GLENN VAN NIMWEGEN

Blue flag iris is a June delight along Acadia's coast.

GLENN VAN NIMWEGEN

Black chokeberry thrives in crevice communities on Acadia's mountains. Narrow cracks in the granite hold both soil and water, providing life on the otherwise barren granite. These communities are among Acadia's most fragile – easily trampled and slow to recover.

ROBERT THAYER

A common sight in bog communities is the pitcher plant. Soil in bogs is deficient in nitrogen – pitcher plants make up the difference by capturing and digesting unwary insects lured into the cones. The bogs are depressions in the bedrock filled with dirt left behind when the glaciers melted away.

Look for Indian pipe, a flowering plant without chlorophyll, in Acadia's woods. The "ghost flower" blooms throughout the summer.

Summer visitors often miss the spectacular lupine bloom in early June. We think of the lupine as an integral part of early summer in Maine – it is a transplant from the Pacific Northwest.

Ferns abound – young interrupted ferns breaking through pine duff and polypody ferns along the delightful Valley Trail on the east side of Beech Mountain—a cool, shady wonderland of tumbled boulders covered with lichen and fern.

ROBERT THAYER

Snowshoe hares are white in winter, brown in summer – protection against the hungry foxes and coyotes that prowl the island.

ROBERT THAYER

Whitetail deer are abundant but seldom seen. Forest, meadow, and pond provide cover, food, and water. A few moose also live on Mount Desert Island.

Acadia's animals are those of the eastern woodlands. Their fortunes are linked to their changing environment. Some changes are natural. Deer and beaver populations increased after the 1947 fire, but have declined since then. Many visitors are disappointed because they don't see much in the way of wildlife. Acadia's wildlife is good at avoiding people and blending into the foliage. Often the visible wildlife—especially raccoons and foxes are visible because they have adopted the panhandling way of life, bad for the animals and potentially harmful to people. For the present, Acadia's wildlife and their habitats appear to be in good condition.

Balance
of Life

ROBERT THAYER

Maine's most abundant reptile, the small common garter snake is most often seen lying in the sun on a trail. There are no poisonous snakes in the park.

GLENN VAN NIMWEGEN

Beaver lodges dot the small ponds. Aspen and birch are the beavers' favorite food, and their favorite building materials for dams and lodges. Beaver mate for life. Youngsters spend two years at home, and then they head off to build their own homes. On Mount Desert Island this causes problems. Roads, carriage roads, trails, and buildings are everywhere – the National Park Service monitors beaver activities closely and intervenes when necessary. Beaver ponds are a focus for wildlife – moose, painted and snapping turtles, frogs, muskrats, ducks, herons, and songbirds all enjoy the beaver pond habitat. Beavers are active at night, the best time to visit a beaver pond is in the evening – bring patience and insect repellant.

TED GRINDLE

ROBERT THAYER

Loons nest on lakes and ponds. The birds are almost helpless on land – their nests are right at water's edge.

Overleaf: Otter Cove shelters a lobster boat below mountains slumbering under a blanket of autumn mist. Photo by Glenn Van Nimwegen

GLENN VAN NIMWEGEN

The Edge of the Sea

The intertidal zone has a greater diversity of life and a greater number of individual organisms than any other Acadia habitat. The plants and animals have to be able to withstand immersion in salt water and crushing waves.

Acadia's tide pools provide a view into a strange and beautiful world. Many varieties of seaweed (algae) provide shelter for a profusion invertebrate life.

ROBERT THAYER

Global warming is changing climate water temperatures around the world. With warmer water, southern species such as the green crab have been able to invade the Gulf of Maine.

ROBERT THAYER

Green sea urchins are relatives of sea stars – both with exquisite radial symmetry. Considered a gourmet delicacy in some Asian countries, Maine's sea urchin population was decimated in the 1990s.

ANIMALSANIMALS/ L.L.T. RHODES

At low tide, harbor seals haul out onto seaweed covered rock to bask in the sun. They can often be seen off Indian Point in Western Bay, at East Bunker Ledge in Eastern Way, and on the ledges south of Little Cranberry Island. Once endangered, since 1972 federal law has protected them and now some 30,000 live in the Gulf of Maine.

GLENN VAN NIMWEGEN

Barnacle larvae attach themselves to rocks in the intertidal zone and secrete protective shells. At high tide their shells open and tiny legs scoop food into their mouths.

ROBERT THAYER

The bullfrog's deep "jug-o-rum" is a familiar sound at Acadia's lakes and ponds. The first tadpoles – the new generation of bullfrogs – appear in May, to the delight of young park visitors.

*In 1688 the French governor of Quebec
gave Mount Desert Island to a French soldier,
Sieur Antoine de la Mothe Cadillac.*

Those Who Came Before

About 13,000 years ago the Wisconsin Ice Sheet melted away from Mount Desert Island. Native Americans arrived shortly after.

WABANAKI

Native Americans have lived on Mount Desert Island for thousands of years. Much of the evidence of their presence on the island has been washed away by rising sea level, but shell middens testify to their presence here 5,000 years ago. Middens are heaps of empty clam, mussel, and oyster shells, and broken and discarded ornaments and tools.

The Wabanaki occupied this area when the first Europeans arrived. There were four tribes—Maliseet, Micmac, Passamaquoddy and Penobscot. They spoke the widespread Algonquian language. They lived off the natural resources of the region and the rhythms of their life was dictated by those resources. The Wabanaki called the island "Pemetic"—meaning "range of mountains."

Mount Desert Island was home for Native Americans for thousands of years.

DAVID MUENCH

Native Americans and European settlers came to terms with the rock-bound coast – an uneasy truce. Today the same coast is a source of wonder for park visitors.

ROBERT THAYER

Boulder fields are the debris left behind as a glacier melts. Shortly after the Wisconsinan glacier melted away some 13,000 years ago, the human history of Mount Desert Island began.

American artists began coming to Mount Desert Island in the 1840s. They saw the pink granite coast as a nonpareil example of the romantic North American wilderness. They exulted in the ever-changing moods and colors – their art invited others to the island.

FIRST CONTACT

In the century after 1492, European sailors reached almost every corner of the globe. Many, seeking the elusive Northwest Passage to China, found their way to the Maine coast. We can't identify the first European to arrive at Mount Desert Island. Here are some possibilities:

European fishermen first may have been on the coast of Maine before Columbus.

In 1497 Giovanni da Caboto (John Cabot) claimed North America for England.

In 1524 Giovanni da Verrazano claimed North America for France. He named it *La Cadi* or *L'Acadie*, from a Passamaquoddy word, *quoddy*, meaning "place." The French subsequently called the area of Maine and the Canadian Maritime Provinces Acadia. Estevan Gomez, a Portuguese mariner, could make a good claim for being the first European at Mount Desert Island—he placed the Rio dos Montanos (possibly Somes Sound) on his map. Many of his place names—Saco, Casco Bay, and Bay of Fundy are still on maps today. His name for New England—the Land of Estevan Gomez—did not survive.

We know that Samuel de Champlain was here on September 5, 1604. Champlain was the first known European to have landed here—he holed his vessel on a hidden ledge and was forced to make repairs. The English and the French changed the Native American way of life forever—the English by their warfare against the French and English— the French by substituting fur trade economy for subsistence economy. The Native American population of Maine was decimated and degraded.

The transition from Native American to European culture had begun.

DAVID MUENCH

In 1604, Champlain described the Mount Desert mountains as "original French here" – "nothing but rock." *He was half right – Cadillac Mountain's South Ridge is nothing but rock, and lichens, and blueberries, and pitch pine, and spruce, and . . . The rusticators – the first summer people—followed the artists. They came in summer and missed out on spring bloom and fall color.*

In the 1850s, steamboats began carrying rusticators from Rockland and Portland Down East to Southwest Harbor and Bar Harbor. The Bass Harbor Head Light was built in 1858 to mark the location of the Bass Harbor bar, a hazard for steamships. In all, four lighthouses were built to guide mariners safely through Mount Desert Island waters.

TOM ALGIRE

EUROPEAN SETTLERS

For many years the Maine coast was a battleground between France and England. In 1613 French Jesuit priests determined to found a mission in Acadia to convert Native Americans to Christianity. The expedition found its way to Mount Desert Island and founded their Saint Sauveur Mission, possibly at Fernald Point in Southwest Harbor. The mission lasted only a few months or less. Captain Samuel Argall, Admiral of the Virginia Navy, attacked the mission and destroyed it. This ended the first European attempt at settlement on Mount Desert Island and began 150 years of intermittent warfare between the French and the English.

Collectively called the French and Indian Wars, the conflict almost prohibited European settlement in Downeast Maine. The coast was unsafe for English and French settlement.

In 1688 the French governor of Quebec gave Mount Desert Island to a French soldier, Sieur Antoine de la Mothe Cadillac. Cadillac and his new bride came to Mount Desert Island, but because of the war between France and England, they left and never returned. Later, Cadillac founded Detroit and was the first governor of French Louisiana.

In 1760 the first English settlers came to Mount Desert Island. Abraham Somes and James Richardson settled at the head of Somes Sound. The village of Somesville is named for the former. For some years settlement and development of the island was similar to the rest of the Maine coast. Cutting timber, farming, shipbuilding, and fishing occupied the residents. In 1835-1836 Richard Henry Dana, Jr., made his voyage to California on the brig Pilgrim and subsequently wrote his classic *Two Years Before the Mast*. The Pilgrim was built in 1828 at Hulls Cove on Mount Desert Island.

Mount Desert Island differed little from other communities on the Maine coast.

Maine lobsters, as caught, are generally not red, like we see them when boiled. The greenish-brown color is most commmon although many are black or other colors, blue or yellow, even white!

Storms keep lobstermen ashore but not fog. "The fog is so thick ye cud stick your knife in it to mark the passage back."

Wooden lobster traps are a thing of the past. Today's traps are rectangular wire cages—but the design is the same. Attracted by a bait bag filled with dead fish (or pieces of cowhide), the lobster (a scavenger) enters the "kitchen" through a funnel shaped entryway—the "eye"—which prevents it from backing out. Attempting to leave, the lobster crawls through another eye into the "parlor," which has no exit. The traps are set on the ocean bottom – some 20 to 100 or more feet down in Mount Desert Island waters. The location of each trap is marked by a colored buoy – a different color and pattern (registered with the state) for each lobsterman. Traps are checked at least every third day and may contain several lobsters. In 2008 there were about 67 million pounds of lobster caught.

Acadia's trails and carriage roads provide new enchantment around every bend and through every season. Huckleberries, members of the heather family, provide spectacular fall color.

PAINTERS AND RUSTICATORS

Gradually life on Mount Desert Island changed from farming and fishing to a tourist dominated economy.

Change came to the island in the guise of art. Artist Thomas Cole, a leader of the Hudson River School of Painting arrived in 1844. Fitz Hugh Lane was here in the 1850s, and Frederic Church in the 1850s and 60s. They provided a romantic vision of the wild and noble seascape that was Mount Desert Island. Their portrayal of the island was dramatically displayed in major eastern cities. "Summer people" started to come.

They called themselves "rusticators." They were teachers and ministers, and others who either did not work in the summer or who could afford a summer on the Maine coast. They came seeking the simple life. Boarding with farming and fishing families, they spent their days rocking (hiking), canoeing, and in nature study.

After the Civil War, there were more would-be rusticators than places for them to stay—and the great hotel era began. The first Bar Harbor hotel was built in 1855. Steamship service came to Bar Harbor in 1857. By 1887, there were thirty-six ho- tels on the island, including the Rodick House in Bar Harbor, which had 400 guest rooms.

Artists and rusticators had spread the fame of the island far and wide.

Maple leaves turn brilliant red in autumn. Green chlorophyll is the photosynthesis engine during the summer. In autumn, with failing light, the maple starts to shut down for the winter. The green chlorophyll fades away. Glucose (a sugar) is left behind. Sunlight and cold nights turn the glucose red – a miracle that happens every year, reaching a peak in early October.

Divide and conquer – vertical compression cracks and horizontal load relief cracks divide granite into blocks.

"Old Farm" was the Dorr family estate, where George Dorr entertained and politicked for his beloved Acadia. He invested his entire fortune, and left his estate to the park. With Dorr's approaching blindness in the 1930s, his reduced financial resources, World War II and Dorr's death in 1944, the building and grounds were victims of deferred maintenance—the National Park Service removed the cottage for safety reasons in 1952.

Now the island economy was dominated by the summer colony—the efforts of the residents were devoted to providing for the cottagers, and the money they brought with them to the island.

The western side of the island retained its agriculture—fishing economy. Southwest Harbor retained its character as a Maine fishing village.

Mount Desert Island had become a prestigious summer destination.

THE TRUSTEES

In the late 1800s, wealthy summer people were molding Mount Desert Island according to their own pleasures. They formed village improvement societies to enhance the already considerable beauty of the island, and began constructing trails for easier access to scenic spots. (Waldron Bates is credited with planning and constructing some 150 miles of trail on the east side of the island.)

But threats of logging and development were ever present—intensified by the invention of the portable sawmill. In 1901 Charles W. Eliot, summer resident and president of Harvard University, called a meeting of some of the more influential members of the summer colony. They organized The Hancock County Trustees of Public Reservations—a nonprofit corporation whose purpose was to acquire lands for public use.

(Eliot's action was a memorial to his late son, Charles Eliot, a landscape architect who had formed the Massachusetts Trustees of Public Reservations)

The Trustees were slow to get off the ground. The corporation was almost dormant until 1908, when Mrs. Charles Homans of Boston gave The Beehive and The Bowl to the Trustees—the beginning of Acadia National Park.

COTTAGERS

In the decades on both sides of 1900, Mount Desert Island became a summer haven (heaven) for the wealthiest Americans.

In 1867, Alpheus Hardy of Boston built the first cottage. There were immense fortunes made in America in the years after the Civil War. And gradually, the island became known to these wealthiest Americans. The first cottages were built in and around Bar Harbor. Soon others were being built at Seal Harbor and Northeast Harbor.

By 1890, Mount Desert Island was competitive with Newport, Rhode Island, as the summer social capital. Astor, Blaine, Morgan, Pulitzer, Rockefeller, Vanderbilt, and others all built immense summer "cottages" on the island. (On the coast of Maine, a house inhabited only in the summer is called a "cottage".) Eventually more than 150 cottages dotted the landscape in an ostentatious semi-circle from Bar Harbor to Somes Sound.

Conservation is simply harmony between nature and man.

First constructed by Waldron Bates in the 1890s, improved by the Civilian Conservation Corps (CCC) in the 1930s, the Ladder Trail uses granite stairs to climb straight up the side of Dorr Mountain. Acadia's trails are laid out for all that happens along the way and not for the destination.

George Bucknam Dorr, a wealthy cottager from Massachusetts, was executive officer for the Trustees. The Homans gift galvanized him into life-long action. His first achievement was the acquisition of Green (Cadillac) Mountain, followed by Sieur de Monts Spring and other key locations. The Trustees' stake in Mount Desert Island was growing.

The Trustees' success aroused opposition. Logging and development interests opposed the Trustees and their removal of land from the tax rolls. Dorr recognized that the Trustees could not carry on this battle forever—the solution was a national park. In 1906 Congress had passed the Antiquities Act, by which the president of the United States could, by declaration, establish national monuments on lands owned by the United States government. Dorr felt that the preservation of Mount Desert Isand could only be accomplished by government action—the Antiquities Act was the means. In 1914, the Trustees gave the American people 5,000 acres on Mount Desert Island so that a national monument could be established, providing government protection.

Acadia Becomes a Park

On July 8, 1916, President Woodrow Wilson proclaimed Sieur de Monts National Monument. In 1919, Congress created Lafayette National Park. The name was changed to Acadia in 1929. Naturally, Dorr was appointed to be the first superintendent of the new park.

It was Dorr's plan to involve the wealthy summer community in the development of Acadia National Park. His success led to continuing donations of land and to the construction of the Carriage Roads and the Park Loop Road. John D. Rockefeller, Jr., started summering on Mount Desert Island in 1908. He soon became an integral part of George Dorr's dreams for the island. Rockefeller's donation of 11,000 acres is perhaps his most important contribution to Acadia National Park. He is better remembered for his magnificent Carriage Roads and for his role in

As part of the carriage-road network, on what was then his private estate, Rockefeller constructed huge gates at the two places where the carriage roads intersected public motor routes—at Jordan Pond and at Brown Mountain (depicted here). Attached to each pair of gates, the "gatekeepers house" permitted Rockefeller and his neighbors easy access to the public roads.

creating the Park Loop Road and the Cadillac Mountain Road.

Under Dorr's stewardship, the park grew continually; the Loop Road and the Carriage Roads were constructed; and 120 miles of trail were constructed or reconstructed, providing access to every corner of the park. George Dorr died in 1944 and passed his legacy to the future.

THE GREAT FIRE

The Great Fire of 1947 burned more than 17,000 acres on the island. Summer had been dry. By October, all of Maine was a tinderbox, ready to burn. Fire came to Mount Desert Island on Tuesday, October 21. On the 23rd the west wind swung to the north and the gale swept the island at more than 60 miles an hour—11,000 acres burned in one day. By October 29 more than 55 percent of Bar Harbor had burned. The fire ended the cottage era on Mount Desert Island. Income tax (1913), the Great Depression (1929-1941), and World War II (1941-1945) had taken their toll, the fire was the finish—67 cottages burned.

Acadia National Park was devastated. Blackened snags stood on the mountains where the magnificent evergreen forest had stood a week before. John D. Rockefeller, Jr., funded the effort to clear the unsightly snags—but the park, from north of Eagle Lake past Bar Harbor to Thunder Hole, was seemingly destroyed. The landscape was dead and desolate. Acadia National Park was in ashes.

At Acadia the Great Fire of 1947 was but a temporary disaster.

Deer Brook Bridge curves gracefuly over its namesake. Set into the spandrel between its twin arches is a plain circular medalion bearing the date of the bridge's construction.

TOM ALGIRE

A *carriage road crosses the Stanley Brook park entrance road. The bridge was constructed by John D. Rockefeller, Jr., in 1933, and restored by the Friends of Acadia in 2001, part of the Friends' multi-million dollar effort to restore the carriage roads within the park. The bridges and roads were constructed to the highest standards. Today they are a unique and irreplaceable cultural resource.*

ROBERT THAYER

The Jordan Pond Gate Lodge is the *second formal entrance to the carriage roads. John D. Rockefeller, Jr., loved to drive horse drawn carriages. For his own enjoyment, he began to build carriage roads on Mount Desert Island in 1913. By 1941, he had constructed 56 miles of carriage road.*

DAVID MUENCH

Nature is patient and strong—the miracle of succession happened again. Hikers can still find stumps in the forests. The path of the fire is still evident to the discerning eye—the evergreen forest has not reestablished itself—the burned area is now deciduous forest. But the resplendent beauties of Acadia—the contrasts of granite dome, forest and ocean—have returned.

SUGGESTED READING

Butcher, Russell D. *A Field Guide to Acadia National Park, Maine.* Lanham, MD: Taylor Trade Publishing, 2005.

Coffin, Tammis E., ed. *The Rusticator's Journal: A Collection of articles from the Journal of Friends of Acadia.* Bar Harbor, Friends of Acadia, 1993.

Dorr, George B. *The Story of Acadia National Park.* Bar Harbor, ME: Acadia Publishing, 1997.

Grierson, Ruth Gortner. *Nature Diary of Mt. Desert Island. Mr. Desert*: Windswept House Publishers, 1992.

——.*Acadia National Park: Wildlife Watcher's Guide.* Minocqua, WI: NorthWord Press, 1995.

Perrin, Steve. *Acadia: The Soul of a National Park.* Bar Harbor, ME: Earthling Press, 1998.

St. Germain, Tom and Saunders, Jay. *Trails of History: The Story of Mount Desert Island's paths from*

The autumn view from Cadillac Mountain *includes mountain ash berries, the Kebo Valley Golf Club, Bar Harbor, the Porcupine Islands, cruise ships, and the mainland across Frenchman Bay. By the 1880s, Bar Harbor had become the center for summer visitors—a position it still holds.*

VICTOR VAN KEUREN

George Dorr built the Homans Path to honor Mrs. *Charles Homans, whose gift of The Beehive and The Bowl was the beginning of Acadia National Park. The trail last appeared on a park map in 1941 and was abandoned for many decades. In 2003 the trail was reopened—a flashback in time to what Acadia's marvelous trails were like when new and unworn.*

Norumbega to Acadia. Bar Harbor: Parkman Publications, 1993.

St. Germain, Tom and Saunders, Jay. *'A Walkin' the Park: Acadia's Hiking Guide.* Bar Harbor: Parkman Publications, 1992.

Thayer, Robert A. *Acadia's Carriage Roads: A Passage into the Heart of the National Park.* Camden: Down East Books, 2002.

——.*The Park Loop Road: A Guide to Acadia National Park's Scenic Byway.* Camden:Down East Books, 1999.

George B. Dorr, "father of Acadia National Park," (left) converses with Charles W. Eliot, president of Harvard University, in this early 1900s photo taken on the shore of Jordan Pond. In 1901 Eliot, Dorr, and other prominent citizens established the "Hancock County Trustees of Public Reservations," an organization whose purpose was to preserve points of interest on Mount Desert for public use. Land bought by the trustees later became a gift to the nation with the establishment of Acadia National Park.

George Bucknam Dorr (1853-1944)

Acadia National Park is the life work of George Dorr. He devoted his life and his fortune to preserving the beauty of Mount Desert Island and making it available to all.

From 1900 until 1916, George Bucknam Dorr, a wealthy cottager from Massachusetts, was the executive officer for the Hancock County Trustees of Public Reservations—the group of wealthy summer cottagers on Mount Desert Island who acquired the first lands that would ultimately become Acadia National Park. Dorr was perfect for the job—personally charming, consummate politician, and in love with Mount Desert Island. Others described him as "eccentric." He was successful in his efforts to get his wealthy summer friends to buy lands to donate to the Trustees—when these efforts failed; he acquired and donated lands bought with his own funds. In addition, he donated lands he had inherited.

George Dorr was indebted to his mother because, while a student at Harvard University, he lost his sight completely. His mother took him to Europe for the finest treatments—medical and psychic! Miraculously, his sight was restored.

Back in the United States, Dorr's mother hoped for a suitable marriage for her son. She was disappointed, he remained a bachelor—the real love of his life was Mount Desert Island. In 1909, after his mother's death, he donated the Beaver Dam Pond and the land around it—*"land in which she had found such happiness."*

By 1914 the Trustees had acquired more than 5,000 acres. George Dorr took the train to Washington to give these lands to the American people. It took all of Dorr's considerable political skills to persuade President Woodrow Wilson that acceptance of the gift and establishment of a national monument were legal and in the public interest. A successful lobbyist, he convinced President Wilson with the help of a Maine senator and congressman, the secretaries of Interior and Agriculture, the president of Harvard University, and Mrs. Wilson! On July 8, 1916, President Woodrow Wilson proclaimed Sieur de Monts National Monument, later Acadia National Park. Dorr was appointed superintendent of the new park at a salary of $1 a month.

As park superintendent, Dorr roamed the

GLENN VAN NIMWEGEN

The Great Meadow lies between
Bar Harbor and Dorr Mountain.
Viewing this peaceful scene today, it is difficult to believe in the Great Fire of 1947,
which burned some 17,000 acres and barely missed downtown Bar Harbor.

mountains—looking for the exciting, the unusual, and the best. Then it was the job of his trail foremen to find ways to put trails where Dorr wanted them—even hanging them on steep mountainsides.

Dorr felt that the names the English settlers on the island had provided did not do justice to Acadia's history and scenery. To this end, he set about renaming Acadia's majestic mountains— Green Mountain was renamed Cadillac Mountain, Newport Mountain was renamed Champlain, and Jordan Mountain was renamed Pemetic—the

Native American name for the island. Many other mountains were renamed similarly. Dorr had renamed Dry Mountain to Flying Squadron Mountain in honor of America's World War I aviators. After his death, it was renamed Dorr Mountain.

Dorr's eyesight failed again in the late 1930s. He passed away in 1944 at the age of 91. After his death, it was discovered that Dorr had not only given his entire life to Acadia National Park, but his entire fortune.

"On behalf of the Hancock County Trustees of the Public Reservations, State of Maine, I have the honor to offer in free gift to the United States a unique and noble tract of land upon our eastern seacoast, for the establishment of a National Monument."

GEORGE BUCKNAM DORR

Acadia is a place of dramatic contrasts—the wind scoured pitch pine and Sand Beach with its multitudes. The beach is one of Acadia's most popular destinations, but because of summer water temperatures below 60 °F, there are few swimmers.

Ocean kayaking has become a popular activity in the waters around Mount Desert Island. Day trips along the Mount Desert Island shoreline and to nearby islands provides another way to experience Acadia National Park.

Acadia is a park for all seasons – the flowers of spring and summer, the berries of August, the colors of autumn, the white winter wonderland. Acadia is a park for all day bird watching at first light, cool forest and sun drenched vista during the day, beaver watching in the evening, and moonrise over Frenchman Bay at night – or listening to an owl or coyote. Acadia is for technical mountain climbers on Otter Cliff and Champlain Mountain, also for bicyclists pedaling up Cadillac Mountain, and sea kayakers paddling to Baker Island. Acadia is for ocean watchers in beach chairs, strollers on the gentle grades of the carriage roads, and for auto tourists on the Park Loop Road. Acadia is a park for all people.

***P**ark rangers are well versed in natural and human* history and provide a variety of talks and guided walks and hikes. Many of Acadia's resources are obvious — rangers help visitors move beyond the obvious to the enchanting.

***A** walk along the Shore Path can renew one's* body, mind and spirit. Glenn Van Nimwegen loved Acadia and enjoyed his walks. He passed away in 2003 but his photography seen in the original edition, live on in this New Version. Glenn was a good friend. —KCDD

***J**ohn D. Rockefeller,* Jr., envisioned his carriage roads as a place where he could escape noisy, smelly automobiles, savor driving his horse-drawn carriage, and enjoy the natural world of Acadia. Today Rockefeller's roads serve a variety of visitors: bicyclers, hikers, walkers, cross-country skiers as well as horse-drawn carriages.

All About Acadia National Park

Eastern National

Eastern National is a non-profit organization that provides quality educational products and services to America's national parks and other public trusts. Eastern National operates educational outlets in over 130 national parks and public lands in 30 states.

Since 1947, they have donated over 65 million dollars to the National Park Service.

For more information, visit www.easternnational.org and www.eParks.com.

Contact information

Mail us at:

P.O. Box 177
Bar Harbor, ME 04609-0177

Call us at:

Visitor Information
(207) 288-3338

Visit us at:

nps.gov/acad

BULL FROG
PHOTO BY
ROBERT THAYER

ACADIA JUNIOR RANGER

Do you want to have fun while learning about the plants, animals, rocks, and history of the park? If so, Acadia National Park's Junior Ranger Program is for you! It is an exciting way for kids of all ages to explore the park's natural and historical wonders.

Go to the Visitor Center, Nature Center or one of the campgrounds to purchase a Junior Ranger booklet. Complete your age appropriate activities, attend a Ranger led program and then have a Park Ranger sign off your booklet to receive your Junior Ranger badge or pin. Wear it with Pride!

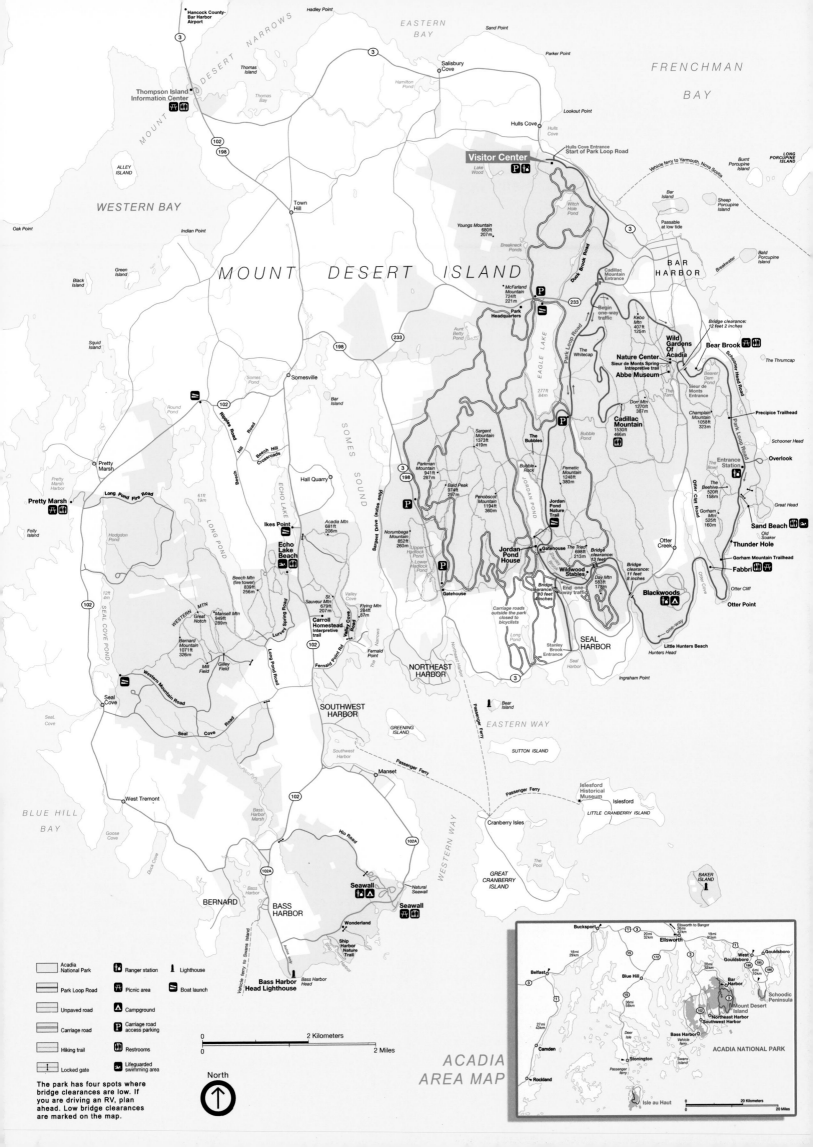

A Look To The Future

Acadia National Park lies within a twelve hour drive to one quarter of the people who live in North America. Every year a little over two million people visit this small (46,000 acres) national park. Almost all come in summer, with another peak during October's fall colors.

With its Loop Road, carriage roads, and 120 miles of trail, it has a tremendous capacity for absorbing lots of people. And those who come here love Acadia National Park—families have been coming to Maine and Acadia for generations. They have been conservationists since before there was a national park—join them by staying on trails, walking on durable surfaces, and leaving nature (including rocks) where you find it.

The best thing about Mount Desert Island and Acadia has always been its people—Wabanaki, farmers and fishermen, boat builders, artists, rusticators, innkeepers, cottagers, and today's residents, park employees, and park visitors. They have always known that this is one of the very special places in the world—a meeting place of granite and sky, granite and forest, and granite and ocean. It has been the job of all to take care of it. And they continue to do a great job.

ROBERT THAYER

Acadia is granite and life. The one is almost indestructible. The other is fragile. Acadia is both – now and forever!

KC Publications has been the leading publisher of colorful, interpretive books about National Park areas, public lands, Indian Culture, and related subjects for over 45 years. We have 5 active series – over 125 titles – with Translation Packages in up to 8 languages for over half the areas we cover. Write, call, or visit our web site for our full-color catalog.

Our series are:

The Story Behind the Scenery® – Compelling stories of over 65 National Park areas and similar Public Land areas. Some with Translation Packages.

in pictures... Nature's Continuing Story® – A companion, pictorially oriented, series on America's National Parks. All titles have Translation Packages.

For Young Adventurers® – Dedicated to young seekers and keepers of all things wild and sacred. Explore America's Heritage from A to Z.

Voyage of Discovery® – Exploration of the expansion of the western United States.

Indian Culture and the Southwest – All about Native Americans, past and present.

We publish over 125 titles – Books and other related specialty products.
Our full-color catalog is available online or by contacting us:
Call (800) 626-9673, Fax (928) 684-5189, Write to the address below, Or visit our web site at www.nationalparksbooks.com

Published by KC Publications · P.O. Box 3615 · Wickenburg, AZ 85358

Inside Back Cover:
Acadia is fog – a soft focus on a hard coast.
Photo by Glenn Van Nimwegen

Back Cover:
Acadia is sunshine, every detail sharp and intense.
Photo by David Muench

Created, Designed, and Published in the U.S.A.
Printed by Tien Wah Press (Pte.) Ltd, Singapore
Pre-Press by United Graphic Pte. Ltd